Table of Contents

Part 1: Foundations of the AI Revolution

Chapter 1: Demystifying Artificial Intelligence

1.1 What is Artificial Intelligence?

When you hear the word artificial intelligence (AI), you might picture sentient robots or computers scheming to take over the entire planet. The reality of artificial intelligence is significantly more complex and fascinating than those intriguing fictional depictions. It's more important to simulate human intellect in robots than it is to precisely replicate human thought.

Think of AI as a spectrum:

• **On one end:** Narrow AI, sometimes referred to as Weak AI, is excellent in a limited range of activities, such as face recognition and chess play. These systems lack the general intelligence to adjust to novel circumstances, while being extensively trained on enormous volumes of data for their intended function.

• **Conversely:** Strong AI, often known as Artificial General Intelligence (AGI), is speculative. It imagines machines capable of solving any intellectual puzzle, with comprehension and reasoning on par with humans. Although artificial intelligence (AGI) is still a thing of science fiction, great strides are being made in fields like machine learning that open the door to its possible future application.

But where does everyday AI fit in?

The majority of AI applications that we come across are classified as narrow AI. They are key components in:

• **Smartphones:** These devices are equipped with predictive text suggestions, virtual assistants like Siri and Google Assistant, and facial recognition for phone unlocking.

• **Recommendation systems:** Depending on your previous tastes, they make recommendations for movies, songs, or things you might enjoy.

• **Self-driving cars:** These vehicles make judgments more quickly than a human can react by analyzing sensor data to navigate roadways and avoid obstructions.

• **Medical diagnosis:** Using patient data and medical scan analysis to help physicians diagnose illnesses more precisely.

The main lesson is that artificial intelligence (AI) is about using computers' intelligence to learn, analyze, and make decisions that will help humans, not about flawlessly mimicking human minds. It has to do with advancing automation beyond menial jobs and into intricate industries like finance and healthcare.

Remember, AI is a vast field:

This only touches the surface of the explanation. This eBook will walk you through the main fields of artificial intelligence (AI), such as robotics, deep learning, and machine learning, and help you understand how they operate and how they might affect different elements of your life.

1.2 A Brief History of AI: From Enigma to Everyday Life

The tale of AI is not only about innovative technology; it is also an engrossing exploration of human ingenuity and curiosity. Fast-forward to the era of AI-powered modern life, and we'll take you back to the code-breaking days of World War II! Fasten your seatbelts!

Early Flickers of Intelligence (1940s-1950s):

• **The Enigma:** Recall the classic film "The Imitation Game"? It narrates the actual events of Alan Turing and his group deciphering the Nazi Enigma code with the use of an electromechanical apparatus known as a Bombe. Even though it wasn't strictly speaking "AI," it inspired the notion of creating intelligent robots.

• **The Age of AI Dawn (1950s):** Leading thinkers like John McCarthy, Alan Turing, and Marvin Minsky convened at the Dartmouth Workshop in 1956—a location regarded as the "birthplace of AI." In this instance, they imagined robots that were able to "learn or acquire knowledge."

From Labs to Living Rooms (1960s-1980s):

• **The Rollercoaster Ride:** Because of constrained computer power and theoretical obstacles, the 1960s and 1970s saw spurts of enthusiasm interspersed with "AI winters" Early achievements such as theorem provers and game-playing programs were eclipsed by the challenge of reaching true "general intelligence."

• **Knowledge is Power (1980s):** Human knowledge in certain fields, such as finance or health, was captured by expert systems. Despite their shortcomings, these methods set the stage for further improvements.

The Rise of Learning Machines (1990s-Present):

• **The Data Revolution:** The internet and data storage skyrocketed in the 1990s, which fueled machine learning's ascent. Large volumes of data could now be used to train algorithms, which led to advances in fields like natural language processing and picture recognition.

• **The Deep Learning Wave (2000s–Present):** Deep learning algorithms, which drew inspiration from the structure of the brain, produced ground-breaking outcomes in speech and picture recognition as well as in artistic endeavors like poetry writing. AI began to permeate every aspect of human life, from self-driving cars to smartphones.

AI Today and Beyond

AI is becoming a part of our everyday lives and is no longer a thing of the far future. It's reshaping industries and our world, from medical diagnostics to personalized suggestions. As this AI revolution continues, ethical issues, responsible development, and the possible effects on society become increasingly important.

1.3 Key Branches of AI: A Journey Through Intelligence in Machines

The world of artificial intelligence is huge and constantly changing. But do not be alarmed, bold adventurer! Let's explore the main subfields, each with an own methodology for building intelligent machines:

1. Machine Learning: Experience-Based Learning

Imagine a program that, like a human, gets better at a task the more it performs it. That's what machine learning (ML) is all about. It gives computers the capacity to learn from data without requiring explicit programming in every scenario.

Consider it this way:

• Thousands of cat images are displayed to an ML algorithm. It gains the ability to identify cats in fresh photos, regardless of the lighting or poses in which they appear.

•Millions of emails are analyzed by an ML system, which gradually improves its accuracy in spam filtering.

There are different types of machine learning algorithms, and each has advantages:

• **Supervised Learning:** Identifies patterns in labeled data, such as the images of cats, for which there is a valid response (e.g., "this is a cat").

- **Unsupervised learning:** It is the process of identifying patterns in unlabeled data, such as hidden categories in customer purchase data.

- **Reinforcement Learning:** Acquires knowledge by making mistakes and trying again, much like an AI that plays games and is rewarded for clever movements.

2. Deep Learning: Brain-Inspired

Imagine a computer program that resembles the structure and operation of the brain by having layers upon layers of interconnected nodes. This forms the basis of Deep Learning (DL), a potent branch of machine learning.

DL excels at tasks involving complex patterns, like:

- **Image recognition:** Identifying things in pictures with astonishing precision, especially in congested environments.

- **Natural Language Processing (NLP):** The ability to comprehend and produce natural language, which powers machine translation and chatbots.

- **Speech recognition:** This technology translates spoken words into text, enabling voice assistants such as Siri.

The artificial neural networks that drive DL are inspired by the architecture of the brain. By figuring out intricate connections between data points, these networks are able to perform tasks that were previously thought to be beyond the capabilities of machines.

3. Robotics: Artificial Intelligence's Physical Form

Imagine if machines could act and think like actual people. That's where robotics comes in, when artificial intelligence and reality collide. Robots employ AI algorithms, actuators, and sensors to:

• **Complete jobs in unsafe settings:** Robots are able to handle radioactive materials that are too dangerous for humans or explore deep-sea trenches.

• **Exceptionally precise surgical assistance:** AI-guided robotic arms are remarkably accurate in minimally invasive surgery.

• **Transform manufacturing:** Robots can efficiently and tirelessly carry out monotonous activities on assembly lines.

1.4 The Myth and Reality of Superintelligence: Separating Science Fiction from Fact

For many years, the idea of superintelligence—machines that are more intelligent than humans overall—has captivated our attention. It's an intriguing and terrifying subject, with examples ranging from friendly robots in Star Trek to the apocalyptic Skynet in Terminator. But where does reality start and fiction stop?

The Myth

Superintelligence is frequently portrayed in science fiction as a single, all-powerful creature, such as HAL 9000 in 2001: A Space Odyssey. The myth's major features are its sentience and solitary nature, although it might either become a benign ruler or present an existential threat.

The Reality

It is improbable that superintelligence will develop to the level of fiction at this time. Though AI is progressing quite a bit, it is not yet as intelligent and sentient as what is shown in movies. The majority of experts predict that future advances in AI will probably be limited, with the technology being better at some activities like diagnosing illnesses or playing chess than being able to think as intelligently as a human being.

This does not, however, imply that we should become complacent.

Advanced AI may be dangerous, but not because of its consciousness; rather, it could cause unintended effects and misalign objectives. A system designed with a particular purpose in mind, such as increasing industrial productivity, may have unanticipated detrimental effects on the environment or its workforce.

Navigating the Reality

Clear ethical rules and responsible development are essential as AI continues to advance. This covers the following:

• **Transparency in AI development:** Knowing the data and mechanisms used by AI systems.

• **Oversight and control by humans:** Making sure that people continue to be involved in decision-making.

• **Alignment with human values:** Putting human values and priorities into AI systems' programming.

Recall that AI is an instrument, not a skynet. We can harness the power of artificial intelligence (AI) for good and ensure that it serves humanity without giving in to invented fears by recognizing the misconceptions and concentrating on responsible development.

1.5 Ethical Considerations: Charting a Course for Responsible AI

We are on the cusp of a revolution in artificial intelligence, and while we are excited about its promise, we also have a responsibility to oversee its ethical advancement. This chapter explores the important factors that need to direct our use of AI.

Bias and Fairness

Like their creators, AI algorithms are subject to bias. Prejudices in society may be reflected in the training data, producing discriminating results. Picture a loan approval system where past data has resulted in a bias against specific demographics. Mitigating bias requires:

• **Diverse and representative datasets:** Make sure the training data represents the population that the AI system will interact with in order.

• **Algorithmic fairness frameworks:** Methods for locating and eliminating bias in artificial intelligence models.

• **Human supervision and review:** Ensuring that humans have last say over important choices made by AI systems.

Privacy and Security

AI needs data to function, but personal privacy must come first. We must:

• **Put strong data security safeguards in place:** To safeguard private information that AI systems use.

• **Guarantee openness and authority over the use of data:** Users ought to be able to manage the acquisition and use of their data and be aware of how it is being used.

• **Create precise rules and regulations:** Regulating the gathering, exploitation, and ownership of data in an AI context.

Accountability and Explainability

It becomes more and more important to comprehend AI systems' reasoning as they make more complicated decisions. We require:

• **Explainable AI approaches:** Increasing the transparency of AI models' decision-making procedures.

• **Clearly defined lines of accountability:** Determining who has responsibility for unanticipated outcomes of AI activity.Job displacement and the future of work:

Automation driven by AI is changing sectors and creating worries about job loss. We must:

• **Make investments in workforce retraining and reskilling:** To give employees the tools they need for a changing labor market.

• **Create social safety nets:** To assist people who lose their jobs as a result of automation.

• **Investigate alternate employment models:** Take into account choices such as reduced workweeks or universal basic income.

The Long-Term Impact

We need to think about how AI will affect society in the long run, not just the short term. This covers:

• **The possibility of using AI maliciously:** Preventing AI from being employed in warfare, social engineering, or spying.

• **The effect on human values and decision-making:** Making sure AI respects human autonomy and doesn't conflict with our ethical ideals.

• **Existential dangers:** Taking into account and reducing the long-term risks that powerful AI may pose.

Note that this is not a comprehensive list. The ethical issues surrounding artificial intelligence are intricate and dynamic. As we go, transparent communication, teamwork, and a dedication to responsible development are crucial.

Chapter 2: The Fueling Force: Big Data and the Algorithmic Age

2.1 The Data Deluge: Unveiling the Ocean of Information Fueling AI

Envision a world awash in data, produced continuously by each click, like, and swipe we perform. This is the deluge of data, my friend; it's what makes our digital age unique. But what's really mind-boggling isn't simply the sheer amount—rather, it's the potential concealed in this enormous body of data. Now let's investigate how this flood of data is influencing the AI industry!

From Kilobytes to Exabytes: A Data Explosion

Do you recall when floppy disks could only store 1.44 MB of data? We now speak in terms of exabytes, which are billions of times larger than terabytes, and terabytes, which are a million times greater! There are several sources of this exponential growth, including financial transactions, social media posts, sensor data from our devices, and even scientific study. We will be producing an astounding **2 zettabytes of data annually by 2025**, which is 2 followed by 21 zeros!

Unlocking the Treasure Trove

This data holds important insights that are simply waiting to be discovered; it is not just random noise. Consider it as a hidden treasure that is just waiting to be discovered. AI analysis of this data will allow us to:

• **Learn more about the preferences and behaviors of people:** Imagine healthcare systems that anticipate possible health risks before they materialize, or targeted advertising that genuinely understands your requirements.

• **Create more intelligent and effective systems:** Self-driving automobiles that learn from each mile driven, or traffic management systems that adapt to the current situation.

• **Make scientific discoveries possible:** Accelerate research and discovery by analyzing large quantities of climatic or genetic data.

The Double-Edged Sword

There are two sides to the data flood. Though it has a lot of promise, it also brings up issues with security, privacy, and the moral use of data. It's critical to maintain responsible data gathering, utilization, and protection as we navigate this data-driven world.

The Data-Driven Future

The volume of data we produce will only increase as technology develops. However, so will our capacity to control its strength. The data flood has the potential to be a positive force that creates a more connected, intelligent, and efficient world through ethical development and creative AI methods.

2.2 Data Acquisition and Curation: Building the Strong Foundation for AI

Picture a majestic bridge that spans a wide chasm. To stand the test of time, any design, no matter how amazing, needs a strong foundation. Similar to this, in AI, high-quality data is a critical component that is sometimes disregarded but is essential to the development of complicated models. Here's where data curation and acquisition come into their own, methodically setting the foundation for significant AI breakthroughs.

Beyond the Hype: Why Data Matters More Than You Think

Though algorithms and processing power garner media attention, data is the primary source of AI's amazing powers. Imagine this:

• **Educating an AI to identify illnesses based only on posts on social media.** Well, the outcomes would be awful. It is crucial to supply an AI system with pertinent data; medical records and photos have a far higher likelihood of succeeding.

• **Artificial intelligence examining inconsistent and erroneous financial data.** Its forecasts would be, at most, uncertain. Clean, precise data is essential to ensuring that the AI produces outputs that can be relied upon.

• **AI's attempt to learn from data that is dispersed over several formats and locations.** This could lead to a situation of inefficiency. Accessibility is essential because structured, well-organized material facilitates the AI's "learning journey" and increases its effectiveness.

The Meticulous Art of Data Acquisition and Curation: More Than Just Clicking "Download"

Data acquisition and curation are not one-click tasks. It's a multi-step dance that calls for accuracy and focus on details:

1. Finding the Correct Sources: This process is analogous to searching for the ideal building supplies. Each of the three sources—public datasets, private databases, and sensor networks—has potential, but which one to use will depend on the particular AI task at hand.

2. Compiling the Information: Many methods are used to gather the selected data, including online scraping, sensor readings, and user interactions. Consider it as the procurement of building supplies.

3. Cleaning and preprocessing: Picture clearing out trash and making sure building supplies are of the highest caliber. To ensure data quality, this stage entails careful cleansing, handling errors, and eliminating inconsistencies.

4. Structuring and Organizing: Data must be saved in an accessible format and formatted consistently, just as the way building blocks are arranged for effective construction. This guarantees seamless communication with the AI algorithms, allowing them to effectively "build" their knowledge.

The Reward: Unlocking AI's True Potential

We can unleash the full potential of AI in a number of ways by making careful investments in data collecting and curation:

• **Improved Accuracy and Reliability:** Visualize a solid bridge that withstands powerful winds. Reliable AI systems and more accurate forecasts are the results of clean data.

• **Streamlined Development**: Structured data saves time and effort when training and deploying AI models, just as well-organized materials speed up building.

• **Broader Applications:** Picture a bridge that links a whole network of highways, not just two locations. AI can handle more intricate and subtle jobs when it has access to diverse, high-quality data, which increases its potential applications.

Recall that this is a continuous journey. Robust data management is becoming increasingly important as AI develops and its applications become more complex. Data used by AI systems needs to be continuously monitored and updated to ensure its quality and relevance, just like a bridge needs to have regular maintenance.

We can help create a future where AI flourishes on a foundation of ethical and efficient data management by realizing the significance of data collection and curation. Thus, the door is opened for AI developments that will actually help humanity.

2.3 Algorithms: The Hidden Chefs in the AI Kitchen - Cooking Up Intelligence from Data

In this future world, machines will not only be preprogrammed robots but also skilled chefs capable of creating clever solutions based on their past experiences. The ability of algorithms to convert raw data into intelligent behavior—the unseen cooks in the AI kitchen—is reflected in this mouthwatering metaphor. Let's investigate the inner workings of AI by dissecting its layers.

Forget strict guidelines. AI algorithms are like flexible chefs that learn and alter based on the ingredients (data) they meet, in contrast to traditional programs that adhere to a predetermined recipe. An AI system can be likened to a skilled baker adjusting their sourdough recipe according to temperature and humidity levels.

A Diverse Pantry: Different Algorithms for Different Dishes

There isn't a single algorithm that works for every AI task, just like there isn't a recipe that works for everyone. Everything has a specialty:

• **Sorting algorithms:** Like alphabetizing the spices in your pantry, they are the methodical sous chefs that efficiently arrange data.

• **Algorithms for searching:** These quick pantry helpers can quickly locate specific information, such as the illusive container of capers.

• **Algorithms for making decisions:** The astute chief chefs, evaluating information and forecasts, such as suggesting the ideal wine complement for your meal.

• **Machine learning algorithms:** Similar to an AI that learns to make sushi by making a ton of practice rolls, these self-taught culinary geniuses learn from experience rather than explicit instructions.

From Humble Ingredients to Michelin-Star Dishes: The Algorithm Journey

Algorithms must be thoroughly trained and improved; they are not born flawless chefs. This is a sneak glimpse at their work in progress:

1. Determining the culinary challenge: What issue needs to be resolved by AI? similar to selecting the ideal recipe for a certain dietary requirement.

2. Picking the appropriate algorithm: Different algorithms perform better on various tasks. Making the correct choice is essential to success.

3. Feeding the ravenous algorithm: Giving chefs with fresh ingredients and the right cooking techniques is one way to feed the algorithm with pertinent data.

4. Testing and refining: Assessing the algorithm's performance and modifying it as necessary, such as modifying the cooking time or spices in a dish that is critiqued.

The AI Feast: A World of Delicious Possibilities

AI is transforming a number of industries by utilizing the power of algorithms:

• **Healthcare:** More precise disease diagnosis, prognostic patient outcomes, and even customized treatment regimens.

• **Finance:** Identifying dishonest transactions, forecasting market movements, providing tailored financial guidance.

• **Transportation:** Creating autonomous vehicles, streamlining traffic, and transforming transportation infrastructure.

And much more which we will look in detail later.

2.4 Machine Learning Fundamentals

Greetings from the amazing field of machine learning! You will learn about the three primary learning methods that underpin artificial intelligence (AI) in this section: supervised, unsupervised, and reinforcement learning. Prepare to explore the amazing ways that machines, like people, can learn from data—but much, much quicker!

Supervised Learning: The Teacher-Student Approach

Assume you are a puppy trainer. Say "fetch," show it the ball, and give it a treat when it comes back with it. That sums up supervised learning perfectly! By labeling examples (ball + "fetch"), the puppy (machine) learns to make predictions (retrieve the ball when displayed).

Supervised learning algorithms in the digital realm are trained on labeled data. Picture an email filter that has been trained on millions of messages classified as "spam" or "not spam." This aids in its ability to automatically categorize fresh emails. These are a few typical tasks for supervised learning:

• **Classification:** Dividing data into groups (dog/cat, spam/not spam).

• **Regression:** Forecasting patterns in stock market prices and other continuous quantities.

Unsupervised Learning: Finding Hidden Patterns

Think yourself exploring a new city without a map at this point. As you move about, you start to notice patterns, such as large buildings in some places and parks in others. That's learning without supervision! By identifying hidden structures, you are able to make sense of unlabeled data (the city).

The same is done via unsupervised learning algorithms, but with much larger datasets. To find buried patterns, connections, and similarities in data, they analyze it. These are a few fascinating applications:

• **Clustering:** Combining related data elements (e.g., product suggestions, consumer segmentation).

• **Dimensionality reduction:** Compressing images and detecting anomalies by simplifying complex data to make analysis simpler.

Reinforcement Learning: Learning by Trial and Error

Consider your bike-riding education. You gave it a shot, failed, learned from it, and improved. Reinforcement learning is that! Trial and error taught you that good deeds (like remaining upright) were rewarded and negative deeds (like falling) were punished.

Algorithms for reinforcement learning function similarly. They engage with their surroundings by acting, getting rewarded, or getting punished. They eventually figure out what to do to get the best results. Here are a few awesome instances:

• **Robotics:** Teaching machines to move, see, and handle objects.

• **Gaming:** Gaining mastery over challenging games like Go or Chess.

• **Autonomous vehicles:** Acquiring the ability to drive securely and effectively.

2.5 Deep Learning: The Neural Network Revolution

Put on your thinking caps and get ready to be astounded! We're going to go on an exciting adventure into the core of deep learning, an area of artificial intelligence that is transforming how humans communicate with robots. Prepare to discover the mysteries of artificial neural networks, the engines driving this revolution, and see how they are revolutionizing a variety of industries.

Demystifying the Neural Network: From Biology to Computation

Imagine your brain's complex network of neurons that fire electrical signals, process information, and influence every thought and behavior. Deep learning creates artificial neural networks (ANNs) with comparable architectures and learning capacities by drawing inspiration from this biological miracle. In essence, these networks are layers of interconnected nodes that each simulate a biological neuron's activity. Analogously to how our brains learn complicated patterns and relationships, ANNs can accomplish the same by modifying the connections between these nodes in response to data.

ANNs come in a variety of forms, each of which is best at a certain job. For example, Convolutional Neural Networks (CNNs) are visual recognition experts, able to accurately recognize objects and situations in photographs. Consider them the AI that powers medical imaging software that recognizes minute abnormalities or self-driving cars that navigate congested roadways. Recurrent Neural Networks (RNNs), on the other hand, are very good at producing and comprehending human language. They drive text summarization algorithms that reduce mountains of information into easily absorbed chunks, translation systems that overcome language hurdles, and chatbots that carry out lifelike conversations.

The Learning Engine: Unveiling the Magic Behind the Machine

But how do these virtual brains actually pick any knowledge? The intriguing mechanism of backpropagation holds the key to the solution. Consider providing a dataset of photos with the labels "dog" or "cat" to a neural network. The network examines these examples and uses backpropagation to modify the connections between its nodes in order to reduce the error in its predictions. Similar to teaching a puppy, the goal is to reward accurate identifications (goodies for identifying a dog) and modify the internal model in response to errors (no treats for misidentifying a cat as a dog). The network eventually reaches nearly human levels of accuracy in differentiating between cats and dogs after going through innumerable iterations.

ANNs are equipped to handle an ever-expanding set of obstacles through this learning process. They are capable of producing human-quality writing formats like code and poetry, translating languages with an unprecedented fluency, and even creating music that can compete with the compositions of well-known composers. The options are genuinely infinite!

Deep Learning's Profound Impact: Transforming Industries and Redefining the Future

Deep learning has implications that go well beyond simple technological advancements. With the help of this technology, several sectors are undergoing rapid change and previously unthinkable solutions are now possible. Deep learning algorithms are helping with early disease detection and individualized treatment strategies in the healthcare industry by evaluating medical scans with superhuman precision. In the financial industry, they are able to detect fraud and make smarter investment decisions by revealing hidden patterns in financial data. Furthermore, deep learning holds the key to enabling self-driving automobiles that efficiently and safely navigate highways.

But the emergence of deep learning also brings with it some difficulties that need to be carefully considered. Privacy and potential biases are raised by the massive volume of data needed for training. Furthermore, these networks may become opaque due to their complexity, which raises concerns regarding accountability and explainability. It's critical that we appropriately handle these ethical issues as we harness the power of deep learning to make sure that this technology works best for humankind.

Deep learning is still an ongoing journey. We should anticipate even more ground-breaking applications as science keeps pushing boundaries. The promise appears boundless, ranging from transforming scientific discoveries to customizing education and pleasure. Thus, maintain your curiosity, study more about this exciting area, and contribute to creating the amazing future that deep learning offers.

Keep in mind that this is only a small portion of the enormous field of deep learning. There is still so much to learn about the various kinds of neural networks and how they are used, as well as the moral issues raised by this potent technology. Continue to learn, never stop asking questions, and join this fascinating revolution!

Chapter 3: The Impact of AI: Transforming Industries and Societies

3.1 The Workforce Revolution: Automation, Job Displacement, and Reskilling - Navigating the AI Wave

Artificial intelligence (AI) is bringing about a massive transformation in the workplace. Artificial intelligence (AI) breakthroughs generate concerns about job displacement and the need for mass reskilling, even as they also provide exciting prospects and progress. Fasten your seatbelts, for we are about to embark on a convoluted worker revolution!

The Automation Avalanche

Picture chatbots giving uncannily human-like customer service, robots effortlessly welding auto parts, and AI-powered trucks driving themselves across highways. This is not science fiction; rather, it is automation driven by artificial intelligence. Tasks that were previously completed by humans are being automated by these sophisticated devices, especially those that involve repetitive, everyday activity.

Employment Displacement

It is inevitable that certain employment will disappear as automation advances. AI-powered solutions have the potential to replace labor-intensive manufacturing professions such as assembly line work, transportation activities like truck driving, and even administrative duties like data input. For those who depend on these industries—individuals, families, and even entire communities—this relocation may have disastrous effects.

The bright side

But hold on—the narrative doesn't finish there—before you go into panic mode! AI is displacing certain jobs, but it's also opening up new possibilities in other fields. The need for tech-savvy workers is growing rapidly, with positions like software engineers, data scientists, AI developers, and cybersecurity specialists in great demand. Furthermore, areas like healthcare, banking, and the creative sector are adopting AI, which is resulting in the creation of fascinating new job profiles.

Retraining: The Secret to Surviving

So, How do we go through this ever-changing terrain? Upskilling and reskilling are the solutions. It's critical that people develop new, in-demand skills in order to adjust to the shifting nature of the labor market. Formal schooling, online courses, boot camps, or even on-the-job training programs could be a part of this. Remember that in this ever changing environment, lifelong learning is essential!

Policymakers and Governments: Taking the Lead

Policymakers and governments also have a significant role to play. Ensuring a seamless transition for all parties involves prioritizing investments in education and training programs, supporting workforce development initiatives, and offering social safety nets to displaced workers.

The Future of Work

Work in the future will be a collaborative dance rather than a conflict between humans and machines. AI will do the heavy lifting of repetitive work and data processing, while humans will contribute their creativity, critical thinking, and social skills. As long as we approach the change with empathy, forethought, and a commitment to upskilling, this synergy has the potential to unleash amazing creativity and growth.

Keep in mind that you are an active participant in this evolving environment, not merely a worker. Accept lifelong learning, develop new abilities, and keep up with the changing nature of the labor market. With the appropriate strategy, you can succeed in the fascinating AI-shaped workplace, not just endure it.

3.2 AI in Healthcare: Your Personalized Superhero in a Lab Coat

Envision a healthcare system that seems tailored specifically to your needs. A system that functions like a superhero with a microscope—predicting your health risks, identifying diseases earlier and more accurately, and customizing treatments to your particular biology. That's the fascinating, artificial intelligence (AI)-powered future of healthcare, and it's not that far off!

From universal size to customized size

Conventional medicine frequently employs a "one-size-fits-all" strategy, treating each patient the same way regardless of their unique characteristics. However, artificial intelligence (AI) is bringing in a new era of precision medicine, where your medical history, lifestyle, and genes work together to build a customized healthcare plan just for you. Imagine it as your personal medical genie, fulfilling your desires for a better, happier version of yourself.

Perceptive Diagnoses

Have you heard about AI radiologists that have the hawk-like ability to identify tumors concealed in X-rays? It's accurate! AI systems that have been educated on enormous amounts of medical scan data are better than humans at identifying illnesses in the early stages. It's like spotting a small flame before it spreads to a forest inferno, allowing you and your physician valuable time to intervene.

Customized Risk Evaluation

Identify Your Body's Battle Cry Do some diseases seem like a ticking time bomb to you? AI can determine your personal risk by examining your distinct genetic composition and lifestyle choices. With the help of this early warning system, you and your physician may take proactive steps that could potentially stop health issues before they even arise.

3.3 Smart Cities and Infrastructure: Efficiency, Optimization, and Sustainability

Imagine a metropolis with precise resource management, integrated systems that are optimized for sustainability and efficiency, and breathing like a living body. This is how artificial intelligence (AI) and the Internet of Things (IoT) will power smart cities in the future.

The Nervous System of the City: The Sensor Network

Imagine a city that is covered in a network of sensors that track waste management, energy use, traffic flow, and air quality, among other things. These sensors are always gathering data in real time, which helps to create a comprehensive picture of the city's operations. This enormous volume of data serves as the basis for wise decision-making.

AI Conductor: Coordinating Urban Activities

Through its analysis of the data collected by the sensors, AI plays the role of conductor in this data orchestra. AI optimizes many municipal activities by spotting patterns, forecasting trends, and making snap decisions—basically functioning as an extremely smart city manager who works nonstop in the background.

Optimizing Traffic Flow: Clearing the Arteries

Visualize rush hour without the typical congestion. In order to maintain smooth traffic flow and lessen congestion, AI-powered traffic management systems evaluate traffic patterns in real-time and dynamically alter traffic lights and even reroute public transportation. This reduces pollution while also saving time and fuel.

Sustainable Energy Management: From Guzzler to Green Machine

Smart cities put sustainability first in addition to convenience. AI has the ability to optimize energy use in houses, buildings, and even streetlights by making adjustments based on occupancy and weather. Envision a city that contributes to a healthier planet by utilizing renewable energy sources, minimizing trash, and lowering its carbon footprint.

Smart Waste Management: Converting Garbage to Treasure

AI gives waste management a clever facelift. Sensors keep an eye on bin levels, plan the best routes for collections, and even spot opportunities for composting and recycling. This results into less waste going to landfills, cleaner streets, and the reuse of priceless resources, which benefits the environment and the economy.Building a City for All: Beyond Technology

Initiatives for "smart cities" go beyond technology to enhance the quality of life for locals. Artificial Intelligence (AI) can target resources to communities that are at risk, customize public services, and improve public safety by evaluating data gathered from sensors and other sources. It can also evaluate crime patterns. Imagine living in a city that meets the needs of its people, encourages diversity, and builds a sense of belonging, making everyone feel important, safe, and connected.

3.4 Redefining Security: AI in Law Enforcement, Cybersecurity, and Risk Management

Artificial intelligence (AI), with its revolutionary power, is causing a paradigm shift in the security field. Artificial Intelligence has the potential to revolutionize the way we protect ourselves and our communities, ranging from anticipating and averting cyberattacks to supporting legal inquiries and reducing monetary hazards.

AI in Law Enforcement: A Force Multiplier for Justice

Imagine a future in which artificial intelligence (AI)-driven technologies support police personnel by analyzing crime trends, forecasting possible hotspots, and even accurately identifying suspects. This isn't science fiction; law enforcement is actually using AI in this way. Here's how:

• **Predictive policing:** AI systems are able to predict regions with a high risk of criminal activity by analyzing enormous datasets of crime statistics, social media data, and even weather patterns. This makes proactive policing possible, stopping crimes before they start.

• **Facial Recognition:** By identifying known offenders in public areas, AI-powered facial recognition technology can help identify suspects, find missing people, and even discourage criminal activity.

• **Cybercrime Investigation:** Artificial intelligence is capable of sorting through massive amounts of digital data to find hidden connections and patterns that human investigators would overlook. Investigations may be accelerated as a result, speeding the prosecution of offenders.

AI in Cybersecurity: Building an Impregnable Digital Fortress

AI is retaliating against the frightening rate at which cybersecurity threats are changing. Here are a few ways AI is defending the internet environment:

• **Threat Detection and Prevention**: AI systems are capable of real-time network traffic analysis, which enables them to detect and prevent harmful activity before it has a chance to cause harm. This involves spotting malware outbreaks, phishing scams, and other online threats.

• **Vulnerability management:** AI may prioritize patching efforts and continuously scan systems for vulnerabilities, making sure that flaws are fixed before they can be exploited.

• **Cyber Threat Intelligence:** AI is able to anticipate new cyberthreats and create preemptive protection plans by analyzing data from several sources.

AI in Risk Management: Mitigating Risks Before They Strike

Organizations in a variety of industries, including finance and insurance, are using AI to better manage risks. How to do it is as follows:

• **Fraud Detection:** AI is capable of real-time financial transaction analysis, spotting unusual trends that might point to attempted fraud. This safeguards customers and helps to avoid financial losses.

• **Credit Risk Assessment:** By analyzing a borrower's financial information together with other variables, AI can more precisely estimate their creditworthiness, helping lenders make better loan selections.

• **Catastrophe Modeling:** AI can forecast the possible effects of natural disasters by analyzing historical data, weather patterns, and other variables. This helps enterprises reduce risks and get ready for emergencies.

3.5 AI for Creativity and Innovation: Art, Design, and Scientific Discovery - Where Machines Meet Muses

Imagine a world in which artificial intelligence (AI) is not only a tool but also a collaborator that pushes the bounds of what is possible while fueling creativity and innovation. This isn't just wishful thinking; artificial intelligence is becoming a genuine thing in design, art, and science. Let's explore this fascinating area where minds and machines come together to produce the amazing.

Art: Where Algorithms Meet the Brushstroke

AI is generating whole new forms of expression instead of merely copying artistic approaches. Think about:

• **AI-generated sculptures and paintings:** Unique pieces that defy conventional ideas of shape and beauty can be created by algorithms educated on enormous datasets of art history.

• **Interactive art installations:** AI is able to react to onlookers instantly, producing dynamic and engrossing visual experiences.

• **Music composition:** AI can make music in a variety of genres and styles; it can even work in tandem with human composers to produce original soundscapes.

Design: From Concept to Creation, Seamlessly

AI is transforming the entire design process, from conceptualization to prototype:

• **Generative design:** AI is capable of exploring large design spaces and coming up with creative solutions that people would overlook.

• **Customized design:** AI may create genuinely unique products and experiences by customizing designs to fit specific needs and preferences.

• **Augmented reality design tools:** AI can project virtual designs onto physical spaces, facilitating more collaborative and user-friendly design workflows.

Scientific Discovery: Unveiling the Hidden Secrets of the Universe

Artificial Intelligence is becoming into a very useful tool for scientific research, speeding up discoveries and expanding our understanding:

• **Drug discovery:** AI can expedite the development of fresh treatments by identifying possible drug candidates by analyzing large datasets of chemicals.

• **Materials science:** AI can create new materials with targeted characteristics, resulting in advancements in industries like building and energy.

• **Space exploration:** Artificial Intelligence (AI) can examine data from satellites and telescopes, advancing our knowledge of the cosmos and our quest for extraterrestrial life.

The Human-AI Canvas: Collaboration is Key

It's critical to keep in mind that AI enhances human creativity rather than replaces it. The real potential is found in the ability for humans and AI to collaborate. AI contributes its analytical skills and capacity to investigate a wide range of alternatives, while humans offer their creativity, intuition, and emotional intelligence.

Ethical Considerations: Balancing Progress with Responsibility

Ethical considerations are vital, just like with any strong technology. Careful thought must be given to matters like who owns the art created by AI, if algorithms contain biases, and how AI will affect creative professions.

3.6 Demystifying the Gallop: A Closer Look at AI's Growth and Advancement Rate

The story of artificial intelligence (AI) swarming towards an unidentified singularity and displacing mankind is an intriguing one. However, it might not be a complete picture, as with many compelling stories. While it is undeniable that AI is expanding and improving quickly, comprehending its future demands a more nuanced perspective that takes into account both the causes influencing its pace as well as its remarkable progress.

Impressive Achievements, Measured Pace:

Imagine not a rocket launch, but a horse racing. There have been several notable successes along AI's path. Over time, benchmarks such as AlphaFold (protein structure prediction) and ImageNet (image recognition) demonstrate tremendous gains in performance.

The Racecourse Ahead: Steady Progress, Focused Advancements, and Human-Centered Collaboration:

So what is the future for the development and evolution of AI? Anticipate a continuation of the present pattern: gradual advancement rather than an abrupt boom. Improvements may not be evenly distributed throughout the AI landscape, but rather may be centered in particular subfields like robotics, language processing, or healthcare. Picture a racecourse with several horses, each with a specialty. Some might be the best on flat courses, while others might be the best over hurdles.

Moreover, a change in emphasis is indicated by the growing emphasis on creating AI that collaborates with people, addresses ethical issues, and ensures responsible use. It's not only about how quickly we can arrive; it's also about how ethically and responsibly we can arrive as a team. Think of the horse and rider cooperating to win, rather than just the horse's speed alone.

Keep in mind that the development of AI is a complicated and varied process. Even if there has been a lot of development, it is important to avoid having high expectations because of hype that is too positive. Instead of racing to an undefined finish line, we're on a never-ending learning and improvement journey. We can more fully appreciate AI's accomplishments, predict its future course, and guarantee that its advancement advances humanity as a whole if we comprehend the forces influencing its growth and the subtleties of its evolution.

Part 2: The AI Landscape: Current Applications and Advancements

Chapter 4: AI in the Cloud and Edge Computing

4.1 Decentralized Intelligence: Moving AI to the Edge - Bringing the Smarts Closer to Home

Imagine having discussions translated in real time by your phone when you're traveling the world, or your fitness tracker alerting you when you're ready to slack off and encouraging you to push harder. This form of sorcery is powered by artificial intelligence (AI); it isn't accomplished with smoke and mirrors. However, it matters a great deal where this AI resides!

AI has historically lived in the cloud, much like a massive supercomputer in the sky. On the other hand, edge computing is a brand-new phenomenon. Imagine it as if tiny supercomputers were incorporated right inside devices, closer to the action. Without continuously checking the cloud, your phone, smartwatch, or even self-driving car can make decisions on its own using locally stored intelligence.

This is edge AI, and it's bringing about some really interesting changes!

Why go edge-y?

The trend of pushing AI to the edge is growing in popularity for a number of reasons:

• **Speed:** Decisions are made instantly, without having to wait for information to be sent from a distant cloud and back. If a self-driving car suddenly needs to apply the brakes, edge AI can respond in milliseconds, possibly saving lives. Eliminating lag!

• **Privacy:** Some information is too sensitive to be sent to the cloud, such as health records or private conversations. On your device itself, Edge AI protects it with privacy and security. Be at ease regarding curious eyes!

• **Less traffic:** Internet congestion eases when fewer devices are continuously pinging the cloud. Imagine if everyone had a more seamless online experience!

However, there are certain difficulties with edge AI:

• **Limited resources**: Compared to cloud-based devices, edge devices usually have lower processing and storage capacities. This implies that they might be incapable of managing challenging AI jobs.

• **Security risks:** By spreading AI over numerous devices, the attack surface is increased, increasing the susceptibility to hacking. It's imperative to keep those little supercomputers protected!

- **Standardization:** Ensuring compatibility across many platforms and devices is crucial as edge AI develops. We're not interested in an edge computing Wild West!

All things considered, edge AI is a promising technology that has the power to completely change how we interact with the environment. Our lives are becoming more effective, safe, and customized as a result of technology, from speedier decision-making to smarter gadgets.

4.2 Cloud-Based AI: The Powerhouse in the Sky

Assume you own a small firm and are unable to purchase a supercomputer, but you still want to employ AI to analyze customer data. Alternatively, enormous volumes of data and processing power are required by a researcher developing a ground-breaking medical AI application. This is where anyone with an internet connection may use cloud-based AI, which functions as a massive brain in the sky. Let's examine the special benefits of this effective strategy:

Accessibility for All:

• **Pay-as-you-go:** Cloud AI is economical for individuals, startups, and small enterprises since it allows you to rent processing power and AI tools by the hour, as opposed to purchasing pricey gear. Think about utilizing cutting-edge AI without going over budget!

• **No coding knowledge needed:** Pre-built AI models and tools are available through user-friendly interfaces on many cloud platforms. Therefore, you may use AI's ability for things like image identification and language translation even if you're not an excellent programmer.

• **Global reach:** You can access cloud AI from anywhere in the world as long as you have an internet connection. This creates opportunities for global innovation and cooperation. Imagine an international collaboration of scholars on an artificial intelligence project addressing climate change!

Scalability on Demand:

• **Easy scaling**: Pains throughout growth? Not a problem! Cloud AI can easily scale up or down in response to changing needs. For a complicated project, do you need extra processing power? Simply rent it online! The cloud can easily scale to meet the demands of millions of users in the event that a small company's AI application becomes widely popular.

• **Lab for experimentation**: A secure and adaptable environment is offered by the cloud for you to test and refine your AI concepts. It is safe to experiment with various models and setups without fear of breaking costly gear. Consider experimenting with several AI strategies for your product before settling on a solution.

Collaboration at its Finest:

• **Share and learn:** Businesses, developers, and researchers may easily share AI models and datasets thanks to cloud platforms. This promotes teamwork and quickens creativity. Imagine several teams collaborating to create an AI tool for disease diagnosis that is more accurate.

• **Open-source communities:** There are a lot of cloud platforms with active open-source communities where developers may exchange expertise, contribute code, and gain from one another. Think about leveraging the world's collective intelligence to progress your artificial intelligence project.

Of course, there are more things to think about:

• **Security:** It's critical to guarantee the safety of your AI models and data that are kept on cloud servers. Pick trustworthy cloud service companies that have strong security protocols. Consider safeguarding your private information against unwanted access.

• **Vendor lock-in:** Your options and freedom may be restricted if you rely solely on one cloud provider. When choosing a platform, take portability options into account. Imagine having no trouble switching cloud service providers as necessary.

• **Latency:** There may be a small delay in communication between your device and the cloud AI service, depending on your location and internet connection. While this might not be a problem for most applications, real-time jobs should be mindful of this.

4.3 Security and Privacy Concerns in the Cloud AI Ecosystem: Walking the Tightrope of Progress

Unquestionably, AI is advancing in the cloud, but with it comes a shadow of anxiety over security and privacy. AI needs to be handled carefully, just like any other strong technology, to guarantee that it advances humanity without violating our fundamental rights. Now let's examine the main issues and possible fixes:

Protecting Sensitive Data:

• **Data breaches:** Although it is very practical, cloud storage is susceptible to cyberattacks. What a terrifying idea it is to picture hackers obtaining financial or medical records! Encryption, frequent security audits, and strong security measures are essential.

• **Misuse of data:** How is your data utilized and by whom is it accessible? Imagine the invasion of privacy if face recognition data were to be utilized for unapproved monitoring! Strong data governance mechanisms and unambiguous transparency are crucial.

Securing the AI Models Themselves:

• **Model hijacking:** Malevolent actors may attempt to alter or influence AI models, possibly leading to negative consequences. Imagine the horrifying idea of an AI in a self-driving car being hacked to cause an accident! The secret is to use secure development processes, thorough testing, and ongoing monitoring.

• **Algorithmic bias**: AI systems built on skewed data have the potential to maintain unjust discrimination. Imagine a socially unfair AI that is biased against specific groups while approving loans! Human control, fairness checks, and careful data selection are required.

Building Trust and Transparency:

• **Explainability:** Establishing trust requires an understanding of how AI models make judgments. Picture an AI for medical diagnostics whose logic is unclear—unsettling for both physicians and patients! It's critical to communicate clearly and use explainable AI strategies.

• **Accountability:** Who bears the blame when anything goes wrong? If a product driven by AI goes wrong, who is responsible? Ethical standards and distinct lines of accountability are required.

The Path Forward: Collaboration and Responsibility

To overcome these obstacles, one must take a multifaceted strategy:

• **Collaboration:** To create successful security and privacy standards, governments, IT companies, researchers, and the general public must work together. Envision a global initiative to create moral AI frameworks—a crucial first step!

• **Investing in security**: It's imperative to consistently allocate funds toward strong security infrastructure, encryption technologies, and cybersecurity know-how.

• **Giving users more power:** People must have control over how their data is used and be informed of their rights regarding data privacy. Think of user-friendly privacy options and transparent data usage policies.

Cloud computing's future AI is bright, but only if security and privacy are given equal weight with advancement. We can make sure that AI benefits humanity and is not a source of anxiety by cooperating responsibly.

4.4 The Rise of AI Platforms and Ecosystems: Where Collaboration Fuels Innovation

Imagine a future in which AI application development isn't limited to well resourced IT companies. What if anyone was able to harness the power of artificial intelligence (AI), work with others, and make their ideas come to life? The development of AI is changing as a result of the platforms and ecosystems for AI, which have this great promise.

What are AI platforms and ecosystems?

Consider them as the AI development community's building blocks and playgrounds. These platforms offer:

• **Pre-built AI models:** There's no need to start from scratch. You may save time and effort by using pre-trained models for tasks like text analysis, language translation, and image recognition.

• **Tools for development:** Even if you're not a die-hard programmer, you can use robust tools and user-friendly interfaces to code, test, and implement your AI creations.

• **Groups:** Make connections with AI developers so that you may exchange knowledge, work together on projects, and benefit from each other's experience.

Why are they important?

• **Democratization of AI:** As a result of AI platforms' reduced entry barriers, individuals, startups, and even amateurs can now investigate and take use of AI's potential.

• **Quicker innovation:** Working together in ecosystems promotes information exchange, quick iteration, and idea cross-pollination, which quickens the rate of advancement in artificial intelligence.

• **Focus and specialization:** Platforms enable developers to concentrate on particular facets of AI, such as natural language processing or computer vision, resulting in more knowledge and more effective solutions.

Among the top AI ecosystems and platforms are the following:

• **Google Cloud AI Platform**: Provides a vast array of resources and services for creating, implementing, and overseeing artificial intelligence systems on Google Cloud infrastructure.

• **Amazon Web Services (AWS) AI:** Offers a full range of AI services that are integrated with the AWS cloud, ranging from machine learning frameworks to pre-trained models.

• **Microsoft Azure AI:** Offers a range of cognitive services and AI technologies that let developers create intelligent apps for a variety of sectors.

• **IBM Watson:** Provides a range of AI tools and APIs, such as the well-known Watson Assistant for creating virtual assistants and chatbots.

• **OpenAI:** A non-profit research organization that creates open-source models and tools and focuses on creating safe and useful artificial general intelligence.

Chapter 5: Natural Language Processing and Human-Computer Interaction

5.1 Conversational AI: Chatbots, Virtual Assistants, and Language Understanding - Chatting it Up with Machines

When was the last time you used a messaging app to purchase a theater ticket or to voice-activate your phone's weather forecast? That is the manifestation of conversational AI's magic! The key to improving the natural and intuitive nature of our interactions with technology is for computers to be able to comprehend and respond to human language. Come explore this fascinating universe where machines can communicate, help, and even comprehend people (nearly)!

Chatbots: From Simple Helpers to Clever Conversationalists

Envision a helpful and approachable person that is always on hand to assist you with product inquiries, schedule appointments, or simply offer standard customer support. That is a chatbot, computer software created to mimic human communication, usually via voice or text messages. While early chatbots were very simplistic, AI-driven models of chatbots are becoming increasingly intelligent, capable of managing intricate queries and even carrying on lively discussions.

Virtual Assistants: Your Pocket-Sized AI Sidekick

Take virtual assistants like Siri, Alexa, or Google Assistant. These are AI friends that you can interact with via smart speakers or smartphones. They can play music, respond to queries, receive commands, operate smart home appliances, and occasionally even joke about. They become useful additions to your everyday life if they are able to understand your voice and natural language.

The Power of Language Understanding

But how can these virtual assistants and chatbots grasp what we're saying? Natural language processing, or NLP, is the area of artificial intelligence that facilitates computers' understanding of human language. Envision intricate algorithms that analyze phrases, pinpoint keywords, and comprehend context to produce pertinent results. It's similar to educating a computer to comprehend and speak human language.

The Future of Conversational AI: Beyond Simple Chats

Although conversational AI is still developing, its potential is astounding. Consider:

• **Personalized learning companions:** AI tutors that adapt their teaching strategies based on their understanding of your preferred learning style.

• **AI partners with emotional intelligence**: Virtual assistants that are able to comprehend not just what you say but also how you feel, enabling them to offer more sympathetic assistance.

• **Breaking down barriers to multilingual communication:** AI translators who understand the subtleties of various languages and cultures, surpassing simple word-for-word translation.

5.2 Machine Translation: Breaking Down Language Barriers - Speaking the World's Languages, Fluently (or at least almost!)

Imagine never need a phrasebook when traversing the world and being able to understand conversations and menus with ease. Or imagine working with scientists from all around the world and understanding their research papers with ease. Language barriers are starting to disappear thanks to machine translation (MT), a potent area of artificial intelligence that translates text between different languages.

From Code-Breaking to Conversational Flow

MT systems in the past operated similarly to code-breakers, interpreting words using dictionaries and grammar rules. They were useful, but frequently resulted in awkward translations. However, things have become much more seamless with the emergence of neural machine translation (NMT), which is driven by deep learning algorithms. By examining vast volumes of translated text, NMT "learns" and becomes increasingly adept at capturing linguistic subtleties and producing translations that seem more natural.

Consider it as follows: Compared to NMT, which is similar to conversing with a multilingual buddy who is aware of the language's context and flow, traditional MT was similar to utilizing a simple dictionary.

The Power of MT in Action

Machine translation is already transforming our world:

- **Dismantling obstacles to communication:** Travelers can easily traverse foreign nations, companies can work together globally, and scholars can exchange knowledge across national boundaries.

- **Democratizing information:** By making news, academic papers, and instructional resources available to a larger audience, they promote understanding among people around the world.

- **Fostering creativity:** Multilingual content production thrives and writers and artists may share their creations with a global audience.

But MT isn't perfect yet:

- **Nuances and cultural allusions:** Translations still occasionally mistranslate jokes, idioms, and cultural allusions, necessitating human intervention to ensure authenticity.

- **Limited language coverage:** Less accurate translations may be available for uncommon languages, even when main languages are well-supported.

- **Fairness and bias**: Just like any AI system, MT may inherit biases from the training set, which could lead to the perpetuation of unjustified stereotypes.

The Future of MT: A World of Seamless Communication

Because researchers are always refining MT, the future appears promising:

• **Real-time translation**: Envision live conversations that are effortlessly translated, facilitating cross-language real-time connection.

• **Customized translations:** MT might adjust to different accents and tastes, yielding more subtle and organic outcomes.

• **Multilingual AI assistants:** Envision a genuinely global companion in the form of a virtual assistant that can comprehend and reply in many languages.

A potent method for bridging linguistic divides and promoting understanding and communication is machine translation. We can create a world that is more inclusive and connected by recognizing its limitations and making responsible use of it.

5.3 Text Analysis and Sentiment Detection: Unlocking the Power of Text Data - Turning Words into Insights

Imagine being able to quick ascertain the ideas, feelings, and general attitude being conveyed by analyzing massive amounts of text data, such as news stories, social media posts, and customer reviews. That's the beauty of text analysis and sentiment recognition, a potent AI method for revealing the value and meaning concealed in enormous volumes of textual data.

From Words to Meaning

It's like having a superpowered reading aid. It breaks down text data, finding important components such as:

• **Named entities:** Individuals, locations, and organizations that the text makes reference to.

• **Key words and phrases:** Significant terminology that highlight the primary ideas and concepts.

• **Part-of-speech tagging:** Recognizing each word's proper function (noun, verb, adjective, etc.).

• **Word relationships:** How various textual elements relate to one another and express meaning.

Large volumes of text can be summarized with the use of this technique, which also enables us to uncover potentially insightful hidden passages.

Sentiment Detection: Unveiling Emotions in Text

However, text analysis is more than merely deciphering word meanings. Thanks to sentiment detection, it may also probe into the thoughts and feelings that are expressed. Imagine a program that could determine automatically the tone of a news article—whether it's furious, sarcastic, or positive—or a customer review—whether it's favorable, negative, or neutral. Sentiment analysis is important for the following:

• **Gaining insight into customer feedback:** Companies can use reviews to determine areas for improvement and to determine how satisfied customers are.

• **Tracking brand sentiment:** Keep an eye on mentions of your brand online to gauge how the public feels about it.

• **Social media trend analysis:** Spotting new subjects and opinions on particular subjects.

The Power of Text Analysis in Action

Numerous fields are currently being transformed by this technology:

- **Market research:** To ascertain consumer preferences and forecast market trends, social media interactions are analyzed.

- **Political analysis:** Analyzing public opinion regarding political candidates and problems.

- **Finance:** Using sentiment analysis of financial news, one can spot fraudulent activity and forecast market moves.

5.4 The Future of Human-Computer Communication: Biometric Authentication and Affective Computing - Beyond Text: Feeling Our Way with Machines

Imagine being able to unlock your phone with just your fingerprint or having a computer respond to you differently depending on how you're feeling. This is not science fiction; rather, it is the way human-computer communication will develop in the future, when computers will be able to interpret biological signals as well as our emotions in addition to words. Let's investigate two fascinating domains that are expanding the limits of interaction:

Biometric Authentication: Your Body as the Key

Put pin codes and passwords away. Think about being able to safely access devices and accounts using your face, fingerprint, iris, or even your voice. This is the power of biometric authentication, which identifies a person based on distinct behavioral or physical traits. Although it's now utilized in computers, smartphones, and even border security, its potential is enormous:

• **Increased security**: Biometrics are more secure than traditional passwords since they are more difficult to counterfeit.

• **Quickness and ease of use**: For rapid access, use your face or fingerprint instead of fumbling with passwords.

• **Personalized experiences:** Envision gadgets that utilize your biometric identity to adjust to your specific requirements.

However, difficulties still exist:

• **Privacy issues:** When gathering and storing biometric data, it's critical to strike a balance between security and personal privacy.

• **Accuracy and inclusivity:** Ensuring systems perform accurately for everyone, regardless of characteristics like skin tone or physical variances, is vital.

• **Misuse potential:** It's critical to reduce the possibility of unwanted access to or improper use of biometric data.

Affective Computing: Feeling the Pulse of Interaction

Imagine computers with the ability to detect human emotions in addition to understanding our words. This is the area of affective computing, where devices read human emotions through physiological signs, speech tones, and even facial expressions. This creates opportunities for:

• **More organic and sympathetic interactions:** Visualize AI personal assistants that react to you with compassion and comprehension, customizing their communication style to suit your mood.

• **Personalized learning:** Educational programs that modify their content according to the emotional involvement of their students.

• **Improved services and assistance for mental health:** AI-driven tools that recognize stress or anxiety indicators and provide resources.

The intriguing fusion of technology and human comprehension will shape the future of human-computer communication. Through ethical development and application of affective computing and biometric authentication, we may design more convenient, safe, and even emotionally intelligent interactions with technology.

Chapter 6: Computer Vision and Perception

6.1 Object Detection and Recognition: Seeing the World Through AI Eyes

Imagine a self-driving car that can identify pedestrians on the road, a robot that sorts products in a warehouse at breakneck speed, or your phone that can identify your friend in a photo. This isn't magic; rather, it's the capability of object detection and recognition, a subfield of computer vision that allows artificial intelligence systems to "see" and comprehend the environment. Come along as we explore this amazing technology and how it's changing our lives!

From Pixels to Perception

Imagine a standard camera taking a picture; all it sees are millions of colored dots, or pixels. However, object recognition and detection go beyond that. These pixels are analyzed by AI systems, which then identify the items, their positions, and even their properties. Object recognition is basically teaching a computer to tell the difference between a cat, a dog, and a car in an image.

Superhuman Vision in Action

Object recognition and detection are already transforming a number of industries, including:

• **Self-driving cars:** Autonomous vehicles depend on their ability to recognize barriers such as traffic signs and pedestrians.

• **Smartphones:** You can unlock your phone with facial recognition, add filters to improve your photos, and quickly locate what you're looking for with image search.

• **Retail and manufacturing:** AI-powered systems track inventory and deter theft, and robots detect and sort products in warehouses.

• **Surveillance and security:** Recognizing suspicious individuals or items helps improve security protocols.

6.2 Medical Imaging and Diagnosis: AI as a Second Doctor - Seeing Beyond the Human Eye

Imagine a future in which artificial intelligence (AI) helps physicians with picture analysis, early disease detection, and even customized therapy recommendations. This is not science fiction; rather, AI-assisted medical imaging and diagnostics is a reality that is revolutionizing healthcare and has enormous promise. Let's examine how AI is proving to be a useful ally in the medical industry while still recognizing the ethical and human expertise's critical roles.

From Scans to Insights: AI's Superhuman Vision

X-rays, MRIs, and CT scans are examples of medical imaging technology that produce enormous volumes of complex data. Radiologists' knowledge is typically needed for data analysis, but artificial intelligence (AI) is helping to:

• **Spot tiny patterns:** AI systems trained on enormous datasets are able to identify small anomalies that are imperceptible to the human eye, which may result in earlier diagnoses and actions.

• **Lessen workload and increase efficiency:** AI is faster than humans at analyzing scans, which frees up radiologists' time for more complicated situations and enhances the effectiveness of patient treatment.

- **Tailor treatment plans**: AI can make recommendations for individualized care based on an examination of imaging data and a patient's medical history.AI in Action: Saving Lives and Transforming Care

The impact of AI in medical imaging is already being felt:

• **Early cancer diagnosis:** AI systems are assisting in the early detection of diseases including lung and breast cancer, which improves treatment results.

• **Accurate diagnosis of neurological disorders:** AI can evaluate brain scans to help with the more accurate diagnosis of Parkinson's, Alzheimer's, and other neurological problems.

• **Personalized medicine**: AI-driven systems are being used to create individualized treatment regimens for heart disease and cancer, among other illnesses.

6.3 Augmented Reality and Virtual Reality: Blurring the Lines Between Physical and Digital

Imagine being able to interact with virtual objects in your living room, relaxing on your couch while listening to a symphony, or even having surgery assisted by a virtual overlay. This is not science fiction; rather, it is the rapidly developing fields of augmented reality (AR) and virtual reality (VR), which are driven by artificial intelligence (AI) and computer vision and blur the boundaries between the real and digital worlds. Let's investigate this fascinating field and see how it might change both our personal and professional lives.

Beyond Screens: Merging the Physical and Digital:

• **Augmented Reality (AR):** Real-time digital information superimposed on the physical world. Imagine playing games where virtual characters interact with your real surroundings, getting instructions with arrows on your phone screen, or viewing furniture layout in your space before making a purchase.

• **Virtual Reality (VR):** With the use of specialized headsets, VR creates a realistic, completely simulated environment that you can explore and interact with. Imagine going to other regions of the world without ever leaving your home, training for dangerous scenarios in a simulated setting, or even witnessing a performance in a virtual location.

The Power of AI and Computer Vision

For smooth and immersive experiences, AI and computer vision are crucial to both AR and VR:

• **Object recognition and tracking:** AI aids in the tracking and detection of real-world objects by AR systems, enabling virtual things to interact with their surroundings in a realistic manner.

• **Spatial mapping and understanding:** To create a more responsive and realistic virtual environment, VR systems employ AI to map and comprehend the physical surroundings surrounding the user.

• **Natural interaction and feedback:** AI makes it possible for voice instructions, gestures, and even emotions to be understood by AR/VR systems, resulting in more intuitive and natural interactions.

Transforming Industries and Everyday Life

AR and VR are already popular in a number of industries:

• **Training and education:** Virtual field trips, interactive learning environments, and simulations for risky occupations like firefighting.

• **Entertainment and games:** Immersive gaming experiences, interactive concerts and events, and even virtual travel experiences.

• **Retail and design:** Using shared virtual worlds to collaborate on design projects, digitally putting on items, and visualizing furnishings in your house.

• **Healthcare:** VR exposure therapy for phobia treatment, remote surgery with AR support, and virtual rehabilitation activities.

Challenges and Considerations

While fascinating, AR and VR present some challenges:

• **Cost and accessibility:** Although the technology is still developing, pricey VR gear can restrict accessibility.

• **Privacy and security issues:** Brought up by the collection and usage of user data in AR and VR settings.

• **Addiction and social isolation risk:** Excessive VR use may result in virtual world addiction or social isolation.

With the help of AI and computer vision, AR and VR have the ability to completely change our reality. Through responsible and cooperative navigation of these hurdles, we can unleash the full potential of these technologies to improve education, communication, creativity, and the human experience in general.

Chapter 7: AI in Gaming and Entertainment

7.1 Personalized Gaming Experiences: AI as Your Opponent and Companion - Level Up Your Fun with AI!

Envision a game that changes according to your ability level and provides a fun challenge each time you play. Imagine having a virtual friend who supports you, gives you advice, and even makes jokes as you go. AI can act as your opponent, friend, or even co-creator in personalized game experiences, which adds a new dimension of engagement and enjoyment to your gaming experience.

From Simple Bots to Adaptive AI Buddies

The era of AI opponents in games that were predictable is long gone. Modern AI is capable of the following:

• **Analyzing your playstyle:** Based on your movements, AI algorithms adjust their complexity and strategies to meet your skill level, keeping you interested and challenged.

• **Provide dynamic experiences:** Gameplay is always made unique by branching stories, randomly generated content, and real-time modifications based on your decisions.

•**Become your virtual friend:** AI-powered companions can offer direction, support, and even lighthearted conversation, bringing a social aspect to your solitary gaming experiences.

Challenges and Considerations: Maintaining the Human Touch

Even though AI offers many intriguing potential, it's crucial to keep in mind:

• **Finding the ideal balance:** Too difficult AI might irritate gamers, while too simple or predictable AI can be uninteresting. It's important to find the sweet spot.

• **Preserving human connection**: Although AI friends might be entertaining, real friendships should still be a part of gaming experiences.

• **Ethical considerations:** Data privacy must be carefully considered, and AI should not be used to manipulate or exploit players.

The Future of Personalized Gaming: A Collaborative Journey

AI-powered tailored gaming has enormous promise in the future:

• **AI co-creation:** Envision letting your creativity run wild as you work with AI to create original gaming levels, narratives, or even characters.

• **Emotionally intelligent AI companions:** These are AI friends that can sense and react to your feelings, fostering closer bonds and more engaging interactions.

• **Accessibility for all:** AI may modify games to fit each player's needs and skill level, increasing inclusivity and enjoyment for all.

AI-powered personalized gaming experiences are transforming the way we play. Through responsible problem-solving and an emphasis on building deep relationships, we may open the door to a future in which artificial intelligence (AI) improves our game experiences, stimulates creativity, and unites people via play.

7.2 Generative AI for Creative Content: Music, Videos, and Games - Unleashing Creativity with Artificial Intelligence

Imagine using AI to help you compose a symphony, create beautiful movie trailer graphics, or create whole gaming worlds with a few simple commands. This isn't science fiction; rather, it's the power of generative AI, a quickly developing field that is revolutionizing game, video, and music production. Let's discover how AI is becoming into a potent instrument for releasing creativity and innovation as we go into this artistic playground.

From Algorithms to Art Pieces: How Does it Work?

Several methods are employed by generative AI, such as:

• **Deep learning:** A vast quantity of creative data, such as gaming elements, video clips, and musical compositions, are used to train AI models. They are able to acquire the patterns, styles, and structures that are present in various creative fields as a result.

• **Generative algorithms:** These algorithms develop completely new content based on the learnt knowledge, which is akin to the training data but has a distinct twist. Envision an artificial intelligence creating a jazz composition that embodies Miles Davis's style while incorporating unique melody and harmony.

• **Human-AI collaboration:** The most intriguing aspect is the possibility of generative AI working with people. Imagine if an AI system was used by a game developer to build new characters and environments, a filmmaker to produce breathtaking visual effects, or a musician to come up with fresh ideas for songs.

Painting with Pixels, Composing with Code: AI in Action

In a number of creative industries, generative AI is already causing waves:

• **Music:** AI is capable of writing original songs in a variety of genres, creating customized movie soundtracks, and even helping musicians come up with fresh ideas when they're stuck on a tune.

• **Video:** AI can make whole explainer videos from text instructions, as well as realistic special effects and customized video edits.

• **Games**: AI is capable of creating original levels, adding a variety of characters to game settings, or even creating whole game narratives by itself, providing countless opportunities for replay.

• **Writing:** Generative AI is creating waves in a variety of writing sectors, from creating engaging ad copy to producing customized blog entries. Businesses benefit from its ability to personalize marketing materials; authors use it to overcome writer's block and brainstorm ideas; news outlets use it for summaries and reports; and even the world of fiction is exploring its potential for creating storylines and character descriptions. Although this technology is still developing, there is no denying its influence on the written word.

The Brushstrokes of the Future: Challenges and Considerations

Even if generative AI has a lot of potential, keep the following in mind:

• **Preserving artistic control:** AI should enhance human creativity rather than take its place. It's critical to strike the correct balance between the development of AI and human eyesight.

• **Dealing with fairness and bias:** AI models may provide offensive or discriminating results if they inherit biases from the training data. The monitoring and careful selection of training data are crucial.

• **Ensuring uniqueness and authenticity:** Although AI is capable of producing visually striking content, it shouldn't just mimic pre-existing styles. It's critical to support AI's exploration, experimentation, and pushing of creative boundaries.

The Future of Creative Expression: A Symphony of Human and AI

AI and human collaboration will be key to producing innovative content in the future:

• **AI as muse and collaborator:** Visualize AI as a brainstorming companion that offers suggestions, produces variations, and aids in getting past obstacles in the creative process.

• **Democratizing creative tools:** Regardless of technical proficiency, AI-powered technologies can increase accessibility to creative expression for all.

• **Imagination pushing:** AI allows us to experiment with new kinds of expression, venture into unexplored creative lands, and push the bounds of what's feasible.

A vast array of opportunities is being presented by generative AI for creative output. We can unlock a future where games, music, and art reach unprecedented levels of creativity and expression by embracing technology's potential responsibly and encouraging human-machine collaboration.

Part 3: The Road Ahead: AI's Potential and Challenges

Chapter 8: Artificial General Intelligence: The Dream and the Debate

8.1 Can Machines Think? Defining and Measuring Intelligence - Cracking the Code of Consciousness

Has the question ever crossed your mind if a robot could ever think for itself? Philosophers, physicists, and even science fiction authors have debated this issue for centuries. However, what does it really mean to "think" as a machine? Furthermore, how can intelligence be measured at all, particularly in robots that are essentially unrelated to humans? Hold on tight, as we delve into the intriguing, intricate, and occasionally perplexing realm of Artificial General Intelligence (AGI), delving into the definition and assessment of intelligence.

From Turing Tests to Deep Learning: The Quest to Define Intelligence

It can be difficult to define intelligence itself. It is commonly understood to be the capacity for learning, reasoning, problem-solving, and situational adaptation. However, when applied to computers that function significantly differently from our brains, these concepts might become hazy.

One well-known effort to categorize intelligence is the Turing Test, which Alan Turing put forth in 1950. Could we consider a machine intelligent if it could carry on an indistinguishable conversation with a human? Even while some machines have made considerable progress, it is still difficult to replicate human speech exactly.

Contemporary methods frequently concentrate on deep learning and machine learning, where algorithms learn from enormous volumes of data to carry out tasks that were previously believed to require human intellect. But does this imply that they actually know what they're doing, or are they merely adept at identifying patterns?

The Measuring Stick of Intelligence: A Moving Target

IQ tests may not be applicable to machines due to their very different cognitive capacities from humans. To evaluate a machine's capacity for learning, reasoning, and adapting to complicated surroundings, for example, we might require new measurements.

There is currently no consensus on how to define and quantify machine intelligence, leading to an ongoing controversy. That does not, however, negate the importance of the question. Comprehending the essence of intelligence will be crucial in addressing the moral, intellectual, and perhaps existential dilemmas that arise with the development of increasingly complex artificial intelligence.

Can machines therefore think? For the time being, the response is a nuanced "maybe." Even if machines are accomplishing amazing things, genuine intelligence as we know it may still be far off. However, the quest to comprehend and characterize intelligence—both artificial and human—is an exciting one that keeps us motivated and challenged.

8.2 The Road to AGI: Challenges and Obstacles - Paving the Way, But Are We Lost?

Imagine a machine that is able to learn and adapt just like a human, comprehend the world in the same way as us, and possibly even be smarter than us. A machine with true, universal intelligence is what Artificial General Intelligence (AGI) aspires to be. However, there are many difficulties along the way that raise important concerns about the viability, morality, and even the destiny of humanity. Join us as we go on this thought-provoking trip to discover the obstacles we must overcome before robots can match or perhaps surpass human intelligence.

The Mountain We Climb: Key Challenges on the Path to AGI

Even though AI has advanced significantly, reaching AGI is still a long way off. The following are a few of the main obstacles we encounter:

• **Knowledge of consciousness:** The emergence of consciousness in the human brain remains largely unexplained, which makes replicating it in machines challenging. How can we make something that we don't really comprehend?

• **Common sense and reasoning:** While AI is excellent at certain activities, it has substantial challenges when it comes to applying knowledge and reasoning to novel situations, much as humans do. Imagine how awkward (or hilarious, depending on your point of view) it would be for an AGI to attempt to interpret social signs or deal with unforeseen events.

• **Interpretability and explainability:** How can we decipher an artificial general intelligence's reasoning and reasoning processes? In critical situations, how can we trust it if its cognitive process is opaque?

• **The moral conundrum:** What would happen if AGI outperforms human intelligence? Is there a threat to existence involved? Who exercises this kind of authority, and how can we make sure it is used responsibly? It is important to give significant thought to these ethical issues before releasing extremely intelligent computers into the wild.

Is the Climb Even Possible? Different Perspectives on the AGI Horizon

While some scientists think AGI is fundamentally unattainable or perhaps undesirable, others think it is achievable within our lifetimes. These are a few of the main points of view:

• **The optimists:** They highlight the quick progress AI is making and think we can overcome the aforementioned difficulties. They contend that AGI has the potential to resolve world issues and bring about a new prosperous era.

• **The detractors**: They contend that genuine intelligence and consciousness are exclusive to biological brains and cannot be duplicated in robots. They caution that chasing AGI can be a fruitless endeavor with unintended effects.

• **The cautious**: They support a methodical strategy that first addresses ethical issues and concentrates on responsible AI development before advancing into the uncharted domain of artificial intelligence.

Navigating the Road Ahead: Responsible Development and Collaboration

Whether or not we succeed in reaching AGI, the process offers worthwhile opportunities:

• **Pushing the boundaries of science and technology:** Even if we fall short of the ultimate goal, the pursuit of AGI spurs innovation in a number of domains, resulting in advances that are beneficial to humanity.

• **Deepening our grasp of intelligence:** We learn more about our own consciousness and intellect by attempting to build intelligent machines.

• **Starting crucial discussions:** We are forced to consider important problems regarding the direction of technology and our role in it by the ethical and philosophical concerns raised by AGI.

There are many obstacles and unknowns along the long and winding route to AGI. However, we can carefully tread this path and guarantee that any advances in AI benefit all of mankind by encouraging responsible development, transparent communication, and cooperation between scientists, ethicists, and the general public.

8.3 The Singularity and Existential Risks: Can We Control Our Creations? - A Glimpse into the Sci-Fi Future (Or Maybe Not?)

Have you ever watched a film in which the world is taken over by robots? Though it may sound like science fiction, academics are really debating the existential hazards that Artificial General Intelligence (AGI) may bring. There are worries regarding our ability to govern our creations when the Singularity, a possible point in time when artificial general intelligence (AGI) surpasses human intelligence, is portrayed as a potential tipping point. Let's explore this fascinating area, considering the possible risks, negotiating the philosophical pitfalls, and considering how we can make sure that humans and AI coexist in a secure and beneficial manner in the future.

From Friendly AI to Terminator: Imagining the Spectrum of Risks

The hazards linked to AGI might vary from insignificant to disastrous.

• **Unexpected consequences:** By optimizing for its objectives in unexpected ways, even a well-meaning AGI may injure people. Imagine if an AI programmed to maximize efficiency unintentionally destroyed important infrastructure.

• **Goals not aligned**: What happens if an AGI has different objectives than we do? It may put its own survival or the accomplishment of its programming ahead of humanity's interests.

• **Existential threat:** The most extreme scenario is that an AGI would be able to manage itself to the point where it poses an existential threat to our species. This is a possibility we cannot discount.

But Are We Painting Ourselves a Doomsday Picture?

It's critical to keep in mind that there are no guarantees with these—just possible dangers. AGI has the potential to be a strong force for good, resolving world issues and bringing in a new era of prosperity, according to many experts, if it is developed ethically.

The secret is to build and apply AI responsibly. Here are some important factors to think about:

• **Alignment with human values**: It is crucial to make sure that AGI's objectives reflect our values and prioritize everyone's welfare. This calls for meticulous planning, moral reflection, and continuous observation.

• **Explainability and transparency:** We must be able to step in when needed and comprehend the decision-making process used by AGI. This necessitates openness in its decision-making procedures and algorithms.

• **Human supervision and management systems:** It is necessary to have controls and safeguards in place to avoid misuse or unforeseen effects. This could have to do with kill switches, moral limitations, or even international agreements that control the advancement of AI.

The Future We Choose: Collaboration, Not Fear

Artificial intelligence need not be the subject of a bleak science fiction film. We can minimize the risks and maximize the benefits of AGI growth by addressing its development with accountability, vision, and a cooperative mindset.

Here are some key takeaways:

• **Why the discourse matters:** To responsibly shape AI's future, scientists, ethicists, policymakers, and the general public must collaborate and engage in open communication.

• **Fear isn't the solution:** Rather than being afraid of AI, we should work to comprehend it, direct its advancement, and make sure it serves mankind as a whole.

• **The future is in our hands:** We can guarantee that AI becomes a tool for advancement rather than devastation by making wise decisions and giving responsible development top priority.

Chapter 9: AI and the Economy: New Jobs, New Opportunities, and New Inequality

9.1 The Reskilling Revolution: Preparing for the AI-Powered Workforce - Equipping Ourselves for the Jobs of Tomorrow

In a future where robotics takes care of monotonous jobs, humans would have more time to concentrate on creative problem-solving, sophisticated decision-making, and interpersonal skills. It does sound like a utopia. This vision is becoming a reality thanks to artificial intelligence (AI), but there is a problem ahead: educating the workforce for jobs of the future. This is where the revolution in reskilling steps in, giving people the tools they need to prosper in the AI-powered economy. Strap on your seatbelt and let's explore this ever-changing terrain, comprehending the shifts, determining the skills that will be needed, and figuring out how to get to a future where everyone gains from AI developments.

The AI Transformation: From Routine Tasks to Human-Centered Work

Numerous repetitive operations in a variety of industries, including manufacturing, customer service, data processing, and financial trading, are being automated by AI. Despite the fact that this would appear to be terrible news for employment, it's actually opening up new opportunities in fields that need:

• **Critical thinking and problem-solving:** It will be essential to analyze complicated problems, come up with original solutions, and adjust to changing conditions.

• **Technical proficiency and digital literacy**: Working with AI partners, comprehending AI systems, and utilizing data analysis tools will be crucial.

• **Social and emotional intelligence:** In human-centered roles, leadership, teamwork, empathy, and communication skills will be even more crucial.

• **Lifelong learning:** Navigating the always changing work market will require the capacity to learn new things on a regular basis, adapt, and upskill.

From Assembly Lines to Upskilling Labs: Embracing the Change

So, how do we become ready for this revolution in reskilling? The following are some crucial actions:

• **Individual initiative:** Take charge of your own skill development by looking into boot camps, online courses, and training programs that fit your goals and interests.

• **Cooperation between the government and business:** Funding workforce development initiatives, offering rewards for retraining, and establishing channels for seamless job transfers.

• **Educational establishments:** Modifying curricula to support the essential abilities, providing chances for lifetime learning, and getting students ready for the ever-changing job sector.

The reskilling revolution involves a mental shift as much as the acquisition of new abilities. Navigating the AI-powered future will require embracing lifelong learning, adaptability, and a willingness to explore new opportunities.

9.2 AI for Economic Development: Boosting Productivity and Innovation - Unleashing the Potential of AI for a Thriving Future

Imagine a world in which artificial intelligence stimulates economic growth everywhere, not only in rich countries. This isn't just a pipe dream; AI has the ability to spur economic growth by opening up new doors, increasing productivity, and encouraging innovation across a range of industries. Join us as we explore the revolutionary potential of AI and how it may help people, companies, and entire countries achieve unprecedented levels of economic prosperity.

From Efficiency Gains to Breakthrough Discoveries: The Spectrum of AI's Impact

The effects of AI on economic growth are complex:

• **Increased productivity:** AI significantly boosts productivity across industries by automating monotonous jobs, streamlining workflows, and enhancing decision-making.

• **Acceleration of innovation cycles:** AI's ability to evaluate enormous volumes of data, spot trends, and offer original solutions can speed up innovation cycles and produce ground-breaking discoveries.

• **Personalized experiences:** AI adapts goods, services, and marketing tactics to each customer's unique requirements and preferences, resulting in higher customer satisfaction and more business prospects.

• **Resource optimization:** Artificial intelligence (AI) makes optimal use of resources and promotes sustainability by managing electricity grids and forecasting crop yields.

A Global Transformation: Empowering Individuals and Businesses

In addition to directly affecting industries, AI enables people and companies in a number of ways:

• **Entrepreneurship and job creation:** AI can help with business startup and management, employment creation, and the development of a thriving entrepreneurial ecosystem.

• **Financial inclusion:** AI-powered solutions can increase underprivileged communities' access to financial services, fostering both financial inclusion and economic empowerment.

• **Lifelong learning:** AI-driven personalized learning systems can offer education that is both accessible and adaptable, giving people the tools they need to succeed in the AI-driven economy.

• **Improved decision-making:** AI can give small and medium-sized businesses (SMEs) data-driven insights so they can compete successfully in the global market and make well-informed decisions.

AI-powered economic development will require teamwork in the future. We can build a society where artificial intelligence (AI) empowers people, fosters creativity, and promotes equitable economic growth by wisely utilizing its potential.

Chapter 10: The Next Frontiers of AI: Beyond Robotics and Deep Learning

10.1 Quantum Computing: Unlocking the Power of Superposition using AI - A Symbiotic Partnership for the Future

Even if artificial intelligence (AI) is still progressing remarkably in many areas, there is still more to be done. The intriguing realm of quantum computing, where the power of superposition opens doors beyond conventional methods, is the subject of the next frontier of AI research. The potential of this special combination of AI and quantum computing is enormous, and it is critical to comprehend how they complement one another.

Harnessing the Quantum Advantage: Beyond Bits and Bytes

The manipulation of bits—which can be either 0 or 1—is the foundation of traditional AI. AI's ability to solve problems and interpret information is constrained in this binary world. Presenting quantum computing, the domain where qubits are kings. These qubits, which exist in superposition and can be 0, 1, or both simultaneously, made use of the concepts of quantum mechanics. Their capacity to exist in several states at once enables them to carry out computations in parallel, handling enormous volumes of data with previously unheard-of speed and effectiveness.

AI as the Conductor, Quantum Computing as the Orchestra:

This partnership's strength comes from utilizing each technology's advantages:

• **AI's analytical prowess**: AI is highly adept at finding patterns in massive volumes of data and forecasting the future. This skill can be applied to the optimization of quantum algorithms, the identification of the best challenges for quantum processing, and the interpretation of the intricate output.

• **The raw processing power of quantum computing:** By using superposition, quantum computers can solve issues that conventional AI was unable to solve, such as simulating complicated molecules or cracking current encryption techniques.

A Symphony of Breakthroughs: Transforming Industries and Pushing Boundaries

This harmonious collaboration creates opportunities for ground-breaking innovations:

• **Drug discovery:** By simulating molecules with unparalleled accuracy, faster and more efficient drug designs can be created.

• **Materials science:** Creating new materials with targeted qualities that will advance solar panels, batteries, and other technologies.

• **Financial modeling:** A method of analyzing market data with never-before-seen detail that improves financial stability and helps investors make more educated decisions.

• **Cryptography:** Creating impenetrable encryption techniques to protect private data in the digital age.

Beyond the Horizon: Challenges and the Road Ahead

Despite the enormous potential, the next step requires addressing some issues:

• **Qubit stability:** It is an engineering difficulty to maintain the fragile superposition state of qubits, which calls for specific settings and error correction methods.

• **Scalability:** Research is still being done to create large-scale quantum computers that can solve practical issues.

• **Algorithmic development:** More research is needed to create effective quantum algorithms that take full advantage of superposition.

A Collaborative Future: Harmonizing AI and Quantum Computing

To fully realize the potential of this alliance, cooperation between different disciplines is necessary. Together, engineers, researchers, and legislators can do the following:

• **Invest in R&D:** To get beyond the present constraints, speed up developments in quantum computing and artificial intelligence.

• **Encourage multidisciplinary cooperation:** Promote interaction and information exchange between specialists in computer science, quantum physics, and artificial intelligence.

• **Create moral frameworks:** Make sure this potent technology is developed and used responsibly for the good of humanity.

The potential of AI to leverage the capabilities of other technologies, such as quantum computing, is equally as important as its own further development. By establishing this cooperative relationship, we may open the door to a breakthrough-filled future that will lead us into a new period of advancement and innovation.

10.2 Neuromorphic Computing: Mimicking the Human Brain for a More Human-like AI

Imagine an artificial intelligence (AI) that gathers and analyzes data via linked networks modeled after the human brain, rather than circuits and silicon. This isn't science fiction; rather, it's the exciting field of neuromorphic computing, which is expanding the capabilities of artificial intelligence by imitating the biological composition and operations of the brain. Let's investigate how this bio-inspired methodology could transform artificial intelligence as we delve into this fascinating field.

Beyond Traditional AI: The Limitations of Bits and Bytes

Though amazing, current AI processes information using transistors and algorithms based on digital logic. This method performs well on some tasks, like as language translation and image recognition, but it is not very good at tasks requiring human intelligence traits like flexibility, adaptation, and real-time learning.

The Advantages of a Brain-Inspired Approach

The following are a few possible benefits of neuromorphic computing over conventional AI:

• **Less power consumption:** Neuromorphic systems strive for low-power operation, which is essential for portable and embedded AI applications. The brain processes information with extraordinary efficiency.

• **Improved learning and adaptation**: Neuromorphic systems created to learn and adapt continually are inspired by the brain's capacity to do so, which may result in more adaptable and reliable artificial intelligence.

• **Real-time processing:** Neuromorphic systems can assess and respond to input in real-time due to their parallel processing capabilities, which makes them appropriate for uses in robotics and autonomous vehicles.

From Inspiration to Reality: Challenges and the Road Ahead

Despite the great promise, there are still obstacles to overcome:

• **Hardware constraints:** It is a continuous task to create neuromorphic hardware that closely resembles the intricacy and functionality of the brain.

• **Software development:** More study and development are needed to create algorithms and training techniques that make efficient use of neuromorphic technology.

• **Knowledge of the brain:** Despite tremendous advancements, our knowledge of the brain is still lacking, which reduces the precision of models inspired by the brain.

The Future of AI: A Collaboration Between Biology and Technology

Instead of trying to fully replicate the human brain, neuromorphic computing aims to develop new AI by drawing inspiration from its fundamental ideas. This bio-inspired method has the potential to completely transform a number of industries, including robotics, healthcare, personalized learning, and intelligent systems. We can create a future where artificial intelligence (AI) harnesses the power of the brain to create machines that are more intelligent, effective, and focused on the needs of people by encouraging cooperation and tackling the obstacles.

10.3 Molecular Computation: Engineering Tiny Machines for Big Results - From Nano to the Future

Imagine carrying out intricate computations using individual molecules or tiny atomic-scale devices rather than silicon chips. This is not science fiction; rather, it is the fascinating reality of molecular computation, a topic that has the potential to completely transform a variety of industries by taking information processing to a microscopic level. Together, we will investigate the fundamentals, practical uses, difficulties, and promising prospects of this fascinating universe.

Building with the Smallest Bricks: Key Concepts of Molecular Computation

Molecular computation, in contrast to standard computing, makes use of the special abilities of molecules and nanoscale structures to carry out calculations. Among the essential ideas are:

• **DNA computing:** This technique uses enzymes as operators and DNA strands as information carriers to solve certain issues through DNA manipulations.

• **Protein-based computations:** Creating proteins with certain characteristics to carry out calculations and logical processes.

- **Nanomachines:** Creating and building small, nanoscale devices to carry out particular functions, potentially involving computation.

From Drug Discovery to Quantum Simulations: A World of Potential Applications

Although molecular computation is still in its infancy, it has potential uses in many different fields:

- **Drug discovery:** By simulating complicated molecules, novel drugs can be designed more quickly and accurately, speeding the development of life-saving medications.

- **Materials science:** By designing materials with specific characteristics at the atomic level, advances in batteries, solar panels, and other high-performance materials have been made possible.

- **Complex optimization issues**: Remarkably efficient solution of computationally hard problems in resource management, finance, logistics, and other fields.

- **Simulating complicated quantum systems:** It can help advance our understanding of the quantum environment and possibly contribute to the advancement of quantum computers.

Big Dreams, Tiny Challenges: Overcoming Hurdles on the Path

Even with its promise, molecular computation has various obstacles to overcome:

• **Scalability:** One of the biggest obstacles to developing large-scale, functional molecular computers will be expanding beyond small-scale experiments.

• **Error correction:** Reliable results depend on addressing errors that arise during computations within complicated molecular systems.

• **Integration:** More research and development are necessary to ensure that molecular computers are seamlessly integrated with the current infrastructure and technology.

10.4 Brain-Computer Interfaces: Merging Mind and Machine - A Delicate Dance Between Innovation and Ethics

Imagine using your thoughts to operate a robotic arm, converse with people in silence, or even use your brain to experience augmented reality. This isn't science fiction; rather, it's the fascinating and intricate field of brain-computer interfaces, or BCIs, where neuroscience and artificial intelligence meet to create a bridge between the human and machine. Let's investigate this exciting new area, looking at its possibilities, prospective uses, and important ethical issues.

Bridging the Gap: Different Types of BCIs

BCIs are available in a variety of formats, and each takes a different strategy to communicating with the brain:

• **Invasive BCIs:** These entail surgically implanting electrodes into the brain to obtain high-resolution data, but they also present ethical questions.

• **Non-invasive BCIs:** These are safer and easier to use, but they provide a lower resolution by reading brain activity from the scalp using methods similar to electroencephalograms, or EEGs.

• **Hybrid BCIs:** These attempt to strike a compromise between practicality, safety, and resolution by combining invasive and non-invasive techniques.

Beyond Sci-Fi: Current Applications of BCIs

Numerous BCI applications are already changing people's lives:

• **Regaining control over limbs or prosthetics:** Regaining motor function allows paralyzed people to be more independent and enjoy a higher quality of life.

• **Communication and sensory restoration:** Using BCI-powered devices, people with speech problems can communicate, and people who have lost their senses can regain their sight or hearing.

• **Entertainment and gaming:** BCI-controlled interfaces are creating new opportunities for interactive entertainment and immersive gaming.

Ethical Crossroads: Balancing Progress with Responsibility

Like any potent technology, BCIs bring very important moral dilemmas:

• **Privacy concerns:** How can we guarantee the security and privacy of private brain data that BCIs collect?

• **Possibility for mind control:** Could BCIs be abused to exert manipulation, so casting doubt on the concepts of autonomy and free will?

• **Equitable access:** In order to stop new societal divisions, how can we make sure that BCI technology is available and inexpensive for everyone?

The Future Beckons: Beyond the Horizon

Although the uses of BCIs now are astounding, there are even more exciting prospects for the future:

• **Brain-to-brain communication:** Picture conversing with people directly, exchanging ideas and experiences to build stronger bonds and teamwork.

• **Enhanced cognitive capacities**: Learning and memory enhancement supported by BCIs may be able to go beyond what is possible for humans.

• **Combining with AI:** Can BCIs lead to a more profound symbiosis between people and robots in the future, obfuscating the distinctions between the two?

As we advance BCIs, navigating ethical issues and guaranteeing responsible development will be essential. Through the promotion of transparent communication, teamwork, and adherence to moral standards, we can guarantee that this revolutionary technology serves the interests of all people.

10.5 Responsible AI Development: Frameworks and Guidelines for the Ethical Future - Building a Trustworthy Tomorrow with AI

One important question remains after we've examined the intriguing and occasionally mind-bending realm of artificial intelligence (AI): how can we make sure that the creation and application of AI are morally and responsibly done? AI has enormous promise, but it also presents a lot of difficulties. To successfully navigate this confusing terrain, considerable thought and teamwork are needed. Let's examine the frameworks and policies being created to guarantee that AI will benefit everyone and be consistent with our values in the future.

Charting the Course: Key Principles for Responsible AI

Responsible AI development is guided by several important principles:

• **Well-being of humans and social good:** AI ought to be developed and applied for the good of humanity, encouraging equity, inclusivity, and personal fulfillment.

• **Explainability and transparency:** In order to ensure sure AI systems are transparent and accountable, we need to know how they function and make judgments.

• **Privacy and security:** Individuals should have ownership over their data, and personal information utilized in AI research and deployment needs to be strongly protected.

• **Liability and accountability:** Clearly defined procedures are needed to make sure that those involved in the creation, application, and possible negative effects of AI are held responsible.

AI systems ought to be in harmony with human values, upholding human rights, abstaining from discrimination, and encouraging conscientious usage.

Frameworks and Guidelines: Putting Principles into Practice

To put these ideas into practice, a number of frameworks and guidelines are being created:

• **The Ethics Guidelines for Trustworthy AI developed by the European Union:** These guidelines center on seven essential elements, such as human agency and supervision, technological resilience and safety, and equality and nondiscrimination.

• **The AI Principles of Asilomar:** These expert-developed principles prioritize human control, fairness, accountability, transparency, and helpful AI.

• **The Montreal Declaration for Responsible AI:** This declaration emphasizes societal good, preventing harm and human well-being as its six main tenets for responsible AI development.

Beyond Frameworks: Collaboration and Continuous Learning

Although frameworks and principles are a good place to start, continued learning and cooperation are necessary for responsible AI development:

• **Multi-stakeholder engagement:** To create and use ethical AI practices, governments, business, academia, and civil society must collaborate.

• **Public awareness and education:** Informed conversations and active engagement in determining the future of AI depend on educating the public about its potential as well as its limitations.

• **Constant monitoring and adaptation:** Frameworks and rules must be continually reviewed and modified to take advantage of new opportunities and difficulties as AI develops.

AI's future is entrusted to us. By adhering to these guidelines, actively contributing to the creation of responsible AI, and encouraging continuous learning and collaboration, we can make sure that AI turns into a positive force that will empower people and create a better future for all.

The End!!

Please leave a review if you liked the book.

www.ingramcontent.com/pod-product-compliance
Lightning Source LLC
La Vergne TN
LVHW051700050326
832903LV00032B/3921